Published in 2013 by The Rosen Publishing Group, Inc.
29 East 21st Street, New York, NY 10010

Photo Credits: **KEY** t=top; l=left; r=right; tl=top left; tcl=top center left; tc=top center; tcr=top center right; tr=top right; cl=center left; c=center; cr=center right; b=bottom; bl=bottom left; bcl=bottom center left; bc=bottom center; bcr=bottom center right; br=bottom right; bg=background

CBT = Corbis; DSCD = Digitalstock; iS = istockphoto.com; N = NASA; SBCD = Stockbyte; SH = Shutterstock; TF = Topfoto; TPL = photolibrary.com

back cover N; **4**bg N; **6**br N; bc, bl TPL; **7**t, tl N; **8**br; br N; bc, tl TPL; **9**c N; **10**t. tr N; **11**bc, c, cl, tr N; **14**bl, br, tl N; **15**bc, br N; **16**b, bl, cl N; tr SBCD; **17**b, cr, tl N; **20**c, cl, tr N; **21**tr N; **24**br CBT; c, cl, tr N; **24–25**bg N; **25**bc, br N; **26** cl iS; b, bl N; bg DSCD; **26–27**tc N; **27**bc, bg N; c TF; bg DSCD; **28**bl SH; cl TPL; **28–29**bc iS; **29**b, br, tr iS; **31**c TPL; **32**br N **7**bl, br, **18–19** Steve Hobbs; **10–11**, **17**br Malcolm Godwin/Moonrunner Design; **12–13** Lionel Portier

All illustrations copyright Weldon Owen Pty Ltd.

Weldon Owen Pty Ltd
Managing Director: Kay Scarlett
Creative Director: Sue Burk
Publisher: Helen Bateman
Senior Vice President, International Sales: Stuart Laurence
Vice President Sales North America: Ellen Towell
Administration Manager, International Sales: Kristine Ravn

Library of Congress Cataloging-in-Publication Data

Einspruch, Andrew.
 Life on a space station / by Andrew Einspruch. — 1st ed.
     p. cm. — (Discovery education: technology)
 Includes index.
 ISBN 978-1-4488-7884-0 (library binding) — ISBN 978-1-4488-7966-3 (pbk.) —
 ISBN 978-1-4488-7972-4 (6-pack)
 1. Space stations—Juvenile literature. I. Title.
 TL797.15.E56 2013
 629.44'2—dc23
                              2011048224

Manufactured in the United States of America

CPSIA Compliance Information: Batch #SW12PK: For Further Information contact Rosen Publishing, New York, New York at 1-800-237-9932

TECHNOLOGY

LIFE ON A
SPACE STATION

ANDREW EINSPRUCH

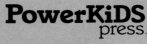

PowerKiDS
press™

New York

Contents

Space Stations Through Time

Not long after people first went into space, they starting thinking about being able to stay up there longer. Travel in a small space capsule was good for a few days, but they imagined how much more they could do with weeks, months, even years in space. Soon they were planning space stations—permanent (or semi-permanent) homes in the sky.

Cosmos 557
Another Salyut scientific space station, it burned up all its fuel once it got into orbit. To hide this failure, the Soviets called it "Cosmos 557" and let it be destroyed by reentering the atmosphere.

Salyut 2/Almaz
The Almaz was a secret military space station, but it was called Salyut 2 to hide this fact. It launched successfully, but, less than two weeks after launch, an explosion ripped off four solar panels. It lost power, crashing soon after.

Dos–2
The Dos-2 was similar to the Salyut 1, but its rocket failed and it crashed into the ocean.

1971

1972

1973

Salyut 1
This was the world's first space station. Launched by the Soviet Union, the cosmonauts spent a record 23 days in space on it. Sadly, the three crew members died while returning to Earth.

Skylab
This was the first US space station, and it supported scientists for 171 days.

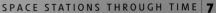

Salyut 3/Almaz
Another Soviet Almaz military space station, this was successfully launched and used by one crew for 16 days.

That's Amazing!
The first space station, Salyut 1, weighed 20.3 tons (18.4 t). The International Space Station weighs more than 18 times as much: 379 tons (344 t).

1976

1975

1974

Salyut 4
This scientific space station hosted two Soviet crews for 93 days.

Salyut 5/Almaz
This was a Soviet military space station that housed two crews for 67 days.

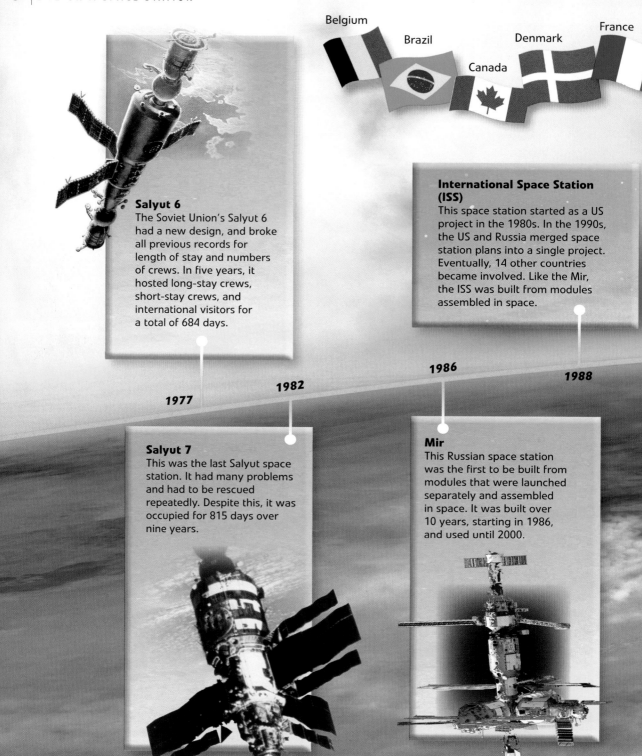

Belgium

Brazil

Canada

Denmark

France

Salyut 6
The Soviet Union's Salyut 6 had a new design, and broke all previous records for length of stay and numbers of crews. In five years, it hosted long-stay crews, short-stay crews, and international visitors for a total of 684 days.

International Space Station (ISS)
This space station started as a US project in the 1980s. In the 1990s, the US and Russia merged space station plans into a single project. Eventually, 14 other countries became involved. Like the Mir, the ISS was built from modules assembled in space.

1986

1988

1982

1977

Salyut 7
This was the last Salyut space station. It had many problems and had to be rescued repeatedly. Despite this, it was occupied for 815 days over nine years.

Mir
This Russian space station was the first to be built from modules that were launched separately and assembled in space. It was built over 10 years, starting in 1986, and used until 2000.

Germany　Italy　Japan　Netherlands　Norway　Russia　Spain　Sweden　Switzerland　United Kingdom　USA

Building the ISS

Space stations are expensive and complex, so it makes sense for countries to join forces and work together on them. The ISS has been built from specialized modules assembled in space.

Year	Name	Country	Purpose
1998	Zarya	Russia/USA	Power, storage, propulsion, guidance
1998	Unity	USA	Berthing locations (connecting module)
2000	Zvezda	Russia	Living quarters, environmental systems, orbit control
2001	Destiny	USA	Research facility, environmental systems, daily living equipment
2001	Quest	USA	Air lock for hosting space walks
2001	Pirs	Russia	Docking ports
2007	Harmony	Europe/USA	Utility hub providing electrical power and a central connecting point
2008	Columbus	Europe	Research facility with laboratory and mounting locations
2008	Kibo ELM	Japan	Experiment logistics module, part of the Experiment Module Laboratory
2008	Kibo PM	Japan	Pressurized module, part of Experiment Module Laboratory
2009	Poisk	Russia	Docking, air lock for space walks, interface for scientific experiments
2010	Tranquility	Europe/USA	Life support, berthing locations
2010	Cupola	Europe/USA	Observation of robotic arms, docked craft, and Earth
2010	Rassvet	Russia	Docking and cargo storage
2010	Leonardo	Europe/USA	House spare parts and supplies
2011	Nauka	Russia	Research laboratory

Getting There

On a space station, people come and go. No one lives there permanently. This means there has to be some sort of spacecraft that blasts off from Earth, docks with the space station, then returns to Earth sometime later. There are two ways of doing this: single-use spacecraft and reusable spacecraft. Both are expensive. The first is a bit like building a car for a single trip to another city. The second requires a durable, multi-purpose truck.

The US space shuttle was an important innovation in space flight. As a reusable spacecraft, it could make multiple trips into space. The shuttle was part bus, part cargo ship. It carried astronauts up and back, as well as their supplies and equipment. The United States ended its shuttle program in 2011.

2

Rocket power
The rockets pushed the shuttle into the sky, working hard against the grip of gravity.

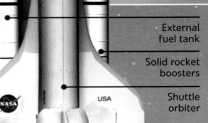

1

Lift off
Six seconds before lift off, the shuttle's main engines fired up. When it was time to go, two solid rocket boosters ignited. These could not be stopped, so they were the last things to fire.

Launch tower

External fuel tank

Solid rocket boosters

NASA

USA

Shuttle orbiter

3

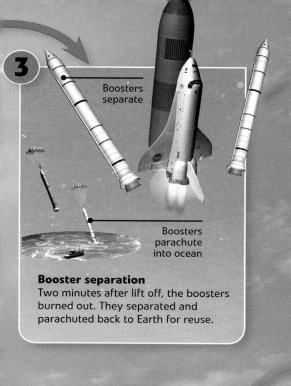

Boosters separate

Boosters parachute into ocean

Booster separation
Two minutes after lift off, the boosters burned out. They separated and parachuted back to Earth for reuse.

4

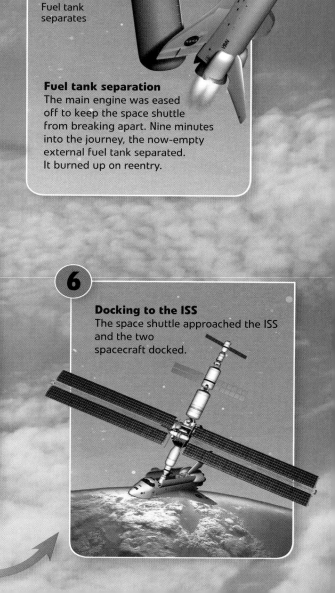

Fuel tank separates

Fuel tank separation
The main engine was eased off to keep the space shuttle from breaking apart. Nine minutes into the journey, the now-empty external fuel tank separated. It burned up on reentry.

5

Reaching space
Ten and a half minutes into the trip, the Orbiter Maneuvering System (OMS) engines fired up. These propelled the spacecraft into low orbit, and thirty-five minutes later, they fired again to get to a higher orbit.

6

Docking to the ISS
The space shuttle approached the ISS and the two spacecraft docked.

How to Be an Astronaut

NASA ASTRONAUT

Candidate prerequisites:

CITIZENSHIP USA

EDUCATION Bachelor's degree in engineering, biological science, physical science, or math

PROFESSIONAL EXPERIENCE At least three years for mission specialist; at least 1,000 hours in jet aircraft for commander or pilot

HEALTH Must pass a NASA space physical examination

HEIGHT Between 58.5 and 76 inches (148 and 193 cm) for mission specialist, or between 62 and 75 inches (157 and 190 cm) for commander or pilot

The men and women chosen to train as astronauts are an elite team of specialists. They have to be healthy, skilled, and experienced. They go through a rigorous training program covering everything from how to live in space to how to survive if there is a problem.

More than a walk in the park
A space walk is a skilled activity that requires extensive training.

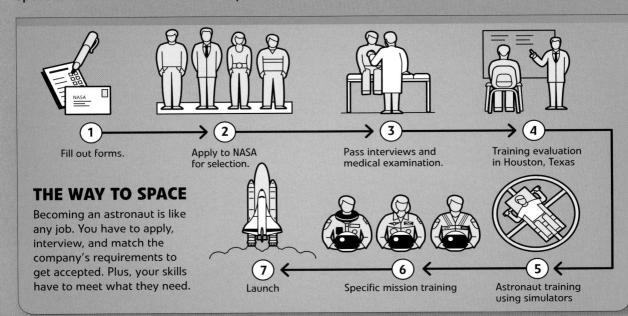

1. Fill out forms.
2. Apply to NASA for selection.
3. Pass interviews and medical examination.
4. Training evaluation in Houston, Texas
5. Astronaut training using simulators
6. Specific mission training
7. Launch

THE WAY TO SPACE

Becoming an astronaut is like any job. You have to apply, interview, and match the company's requirements to get accepted. Plus, your skills have to meet what they need.

Training in weightlessness
Water tanks simulate weightlessness so astronauts can practice tasks before entering space.

Simulated research tasks
This virtual glovebox is practice for handling objects, such as tools and science specimens, while in space.

Emergency exit
Astronauts learn to exit quickly and safely in case of emergency.

Sea survival
If astronauts land in water, they must know how to survive until help arrives.

Shuttle training checklist

☑ Learn shuttle orbiter's systems and use.

☑ Learn space station's systems and use.

☑ Complete Single Systems Trainer (SST) training covering operations of each orbiter subsystem for both normal function and correcting malfunctions.

☑ Work with complex shuttle mission simulators covering all shuttle operations and tasks associated with flight phases, such as prelaunch, ascent, and orbit.

☑ Train with the flight controllers in the Mission Control Center (MCC).

☑ Practice weightlessness in water tanks.

☑ Practice preparing meals, storing equipment, managing trash, using cameras, and conducting experiments.

Daily Life

Living on the ISS makes ordinary things surprisingly challenging. In a free-fall, or weightless, environment, there is no up or down, and everything floats. Activities that people have done all their lives, such as eating, sleeping, and brushing their teeth, are different when stray, floating breadcrumbs can get in their eyes. Muscles become dangerously weak if they are not exercised regularly.

Even using a toilet is tricky. Astronauts have to strap themselves onto it so they do not float off, and a fan creates the suction needed to carry the waste away from the body and into a 5-gallon (19-l) container.

EXERCISING

Exercise is crucial for preventing health problems due to weightlessness. Astronauts exercise using treadmills and bikes, and do a lot of resistance training to keep their muscles and bones strong.

SLEEPING

Instead of a bed, astronauts use sleeping bags attached to the wall so they do not float around, bump into things, and wake up. They must also sleep near an air vent to avoid waking up in a dangerous bubble of exhaled carbon dioxide.

PASSING THE TIME

Astronauts have highly planned workdays. They have to because there is so much to do. A typical day will have two meetings with mission control, 10 hours of work, plus meals, maintenance, exercise, and a bit of free time. One thing is for sure—an astronaut's life is not a dull one.

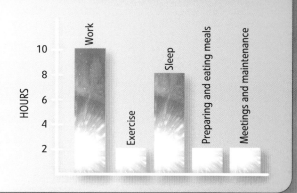

Work

Sleep

Preparing and eating meals

Meetings and maintenance

Exercise

HOURS

10
8
6
4
2

Astronauts need time off, too! On Saturdays, they usually work only half a day, and Sundays are normally a day of rest.

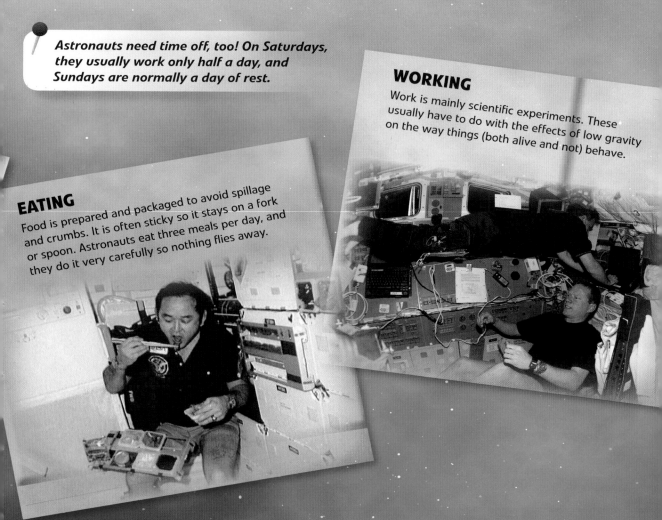

WORKING

Work is mainly scientific experiments. These usually have to do with the effects of low gravity on the way things (both alive and not) behave.

EATING

Food is prepared and packaged to avoid spillage and crumbs. It is often sticky so it stays on a fork or spoon. Astronauts eat three meals per day, and they do it very carefully so nothing flies away.

SNACK TIME

When astronauts get hungry between meals, they will grab a snack. Snacks must be quick and easy, and might include fresh fruits, nuts, pudding, or maybe peanut butter on a brownie.

MAINTENANCE AND REPAIR

If something breaks, whether it is a toilet or an antenna, it is up to the astronauts to fix it. Some repairs require space walks because the repair needs to happen outside the ISS.

EXPERIMENTS

Astronauts conduct many experiments on the ISS, some lasting weeks or months. They look at things such as sleep patterns, the effects of fatigue on reaction times, and how metals and plants behave differently in free fall.

HYGIENE

Astronauts have to keep clean. Some tasks are relatively easy, such as brushing their teeth. But they cannot take baths. On the ISS, the crew use washcloths or moist towelettes to gives themselves a sponge bath.

LEISURE

In their free time, astronauts might check their email, listen to music, read, or maybe write in a journal. And, with a view like theirs, another favorite pastime is simply looking out the window into space and at Earth below.

GROOMING

In space, stray hairs and hair fragments can damage equipment. So, when shaving or trimming hair, vacuum hoses suck away anything that gets loose.

END OF THE DAY

As they head to sleep, astronauts must surely look out at Earth and the millions of stars and simply wonder about the universe they live in.

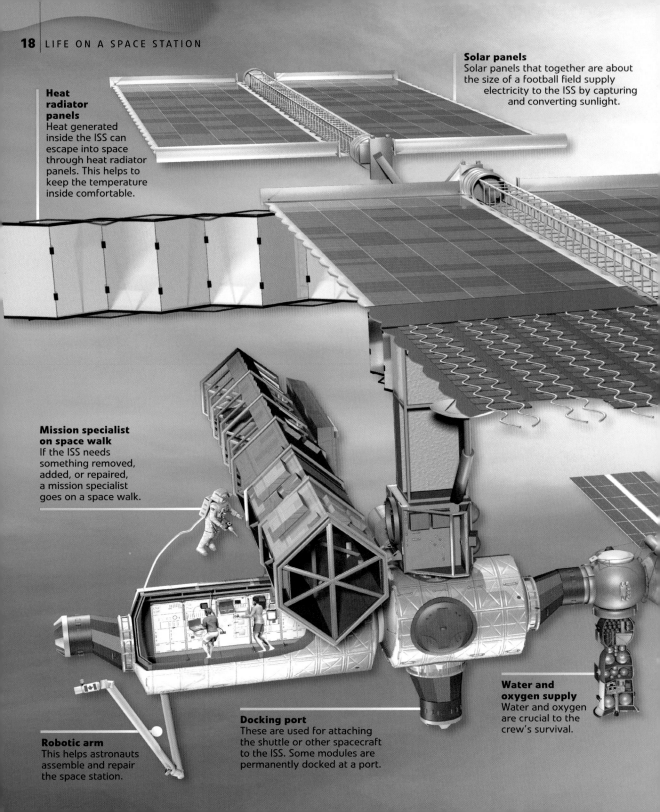

Solar panels
Solar panels that together are about the size of a football field supply electricity to the ISS by capturing and converting sunlight.

Heat radiator panels
Heat generated inside the ISS can escape into space through heat radiator panels. This helps to keep the temperature inside comfortable.

Mission specialist on space walk
If the ISS needs something removed, added, or repaired, a mission specialist goes on a space walk.

Robotic arm
This helps astronauts assemble and repair the space station.

Docking port
These are used for attaching the shuttle or other spacecraft to the ISS. Some modules are permanently docked at a port.

Water and oxygen supply
Water and oxygen are crucial to the crew's survival.

Inside the ISS

> *Whether outwardly or inwardly, whether in space or time, the farther we penetrate the unknown, the vaster and more marvelous it becomes.*
>
> **CHARLES A. LINDBERGH, AMERICAN AVIATOR, 1974**

The ISS is a massive and complex machine that supports human life in the hostile environment of space. A huge amount of technology and skill went into creating a place that would keep humans safe and let them conduct useful research.

Conducting wires
Electricity flows through conducting wires into the ISS from the solar panels.

Living area
This gives crew members a place to gather, eat, and relax.

Sleeping bay
Sleeping places are spread throughout the ISS.

Laboratory
The crew conducts many different experiments in this purpose-built lab.

Air lock
This is where astronauts put on space suits, then go outside into space.

Room to move

Moving around inside the ISS is a bit like moving around inside a bus. There is room, but it is tight and astronauts need to be careful.

Experiments on the ISS

A bove all else, the ISS is used for scientific research. Since its beginning, hundreds of experiments in a wide range of fields have been undertaken. Research has been conducted in human life sciences, biology, human physiology, physical and materials science, and Earth and space science.

Growing plants
Understanding plant growth in space is crucial if people ever want to travel beyond the Moon. Soybeans were grown in the Advanced Astroculture Experiment to see if they would produce seeds, and to see if any of the seeds were different due to the low-gravity setting.

Radiation resistance
What happens when materials have been in space a long time? Do they deteriorate or stay more or less the same? The Long Duration Exposure Facility tested materials, components, and systems to see what happened when they were subjected to space debris and micrometeoroids for five years. These experiments have continued on the ISS.

Since the ISS is in low orbit, just 220 miles (350 km) above Earth's surface, it provides a great view.

Observing Earth

Being able to observe Earth from the distance of space is incredibly useful. The "big picture" view lets scientists observe changes to Earth that happen over time, such as deforestation, soil erosion, and the effects of global warming. This Russian cosmonaut is using a camera with a very large lens to take images of Earth.

Hurricane Isabel

The ISS is the perfect place to watch big weather patterns on Earth. In this photo of Hurricane Isabel, in September 2003, the eye of the hurricane is clearly visible in the middle. Landmasses can be seen in the distance.

Communication
Staying in touch with other astronauts and Mission Control is important. The suit has a cap with earphones and microphone.

Two main pieces
Space suits are made in two pieces (helmet and suit) that lock together at the neck. The upper body of the suit is hard fiberglass with flexible arms.

Backpack
This life-support pack contains oxygen and power supply. It also removes the poisonous carbon dioxide breathed out by the astronaut.

Visor
A gold coating protects against dangerous ultraviolet light.

Control unit
This lets the astronaut control the suit's lights, oxygen flow, and temperature.

Tools
These are attached to the suit so they do not accidentally float away.

Dressed for Space

Not having oxygen in space is the least of the dangers. Facing the Sun, it can get boiling hot, up to 250°F (121°C). Away from the Sun, it is colder than it ever gets in the Antarctic, down to -250°F (-156°C). Without a space suit, the side facing the Sun would boil and the other side would freeze.

Space suits not only have to act like a miniature spaceship, they have to be practical enough for astronauts to get work done while wearing them.

Gloves
Heated gloves are custom-made for each astronaut.

Flexible joints
The space suit is stiff from being pressurized. Flexible joints at the knees, ankles, elbows, and shoulders let the wearer move about.

Space suits weigh more than the human wearing them (although in space, they weigh nothing).

Liquid cooling underwear
The undergarment has tubes that circulate cool water to help prevent overheating.

Space boots
These are part of the space suit to ensure an airtight seal. They have no tread because in microgravity there is no need for traction.

Space Walk Facts

MISSION SPECIALISTS

Only trained astronauts called mission specialists go on space walks. They go outside if something needs to be fixed, removed, or added, and the task cannot be done by robotic arm.

DECOMPRESSION CHAMBER

Before going out into space, astronauts must let their body adjust to the vacuum environment they will experience there. They do this by spending a day in the decompression chamber, which slowly adjusts air pressure.

MANNED MANEUVERING UNIT

This allows the astronaut to move around in space using tiny rocketlike "thrusters." The unit is attached to the space suit and controlled with a joystick. Thrust comes from small bursts of compressed nitrogen gas.

UMBILICAL HOSE

On some space walks, astronauts remain connected to the ISS using an umbilical hose, which also supplies them with oxygen.

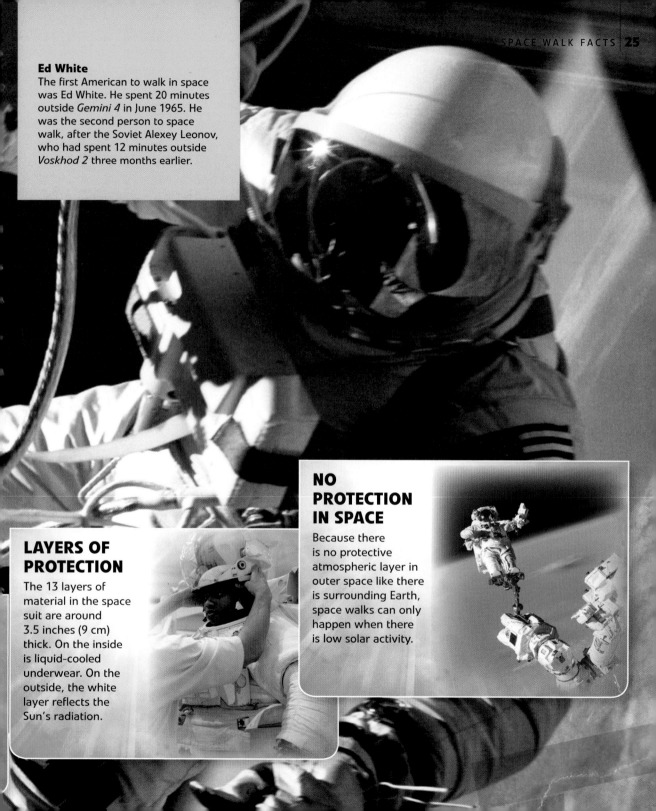

Ed White

The first American to walk in space was Ed White. He spent 20 minutes outside *Gemini 4* in June 1965. He was the second person to space walk, after the Soviet Alexey Leonov, who had spent 12 minutes outside *Voskhod 2* three months earlier.

NO PROTECTION IN SPACE

Because there is no protective atmospheric layer in outer space like there is surrounding Earth, space walks can only happen when there is low solar activity.

LAYERS OF PROTECTION

The 13 layers of material in the space suit are around 3.5 inches (9 cm) thick. On the inside is liquid-cooled underwear. On the outside, the white layer reflects the Sun's radiation.

Space Station Facts

There is plenty of trivia surrounding space stations, with so many different activities, experiments, nations, and facts related to them. Here are just a few of the more interesting and unusual facts we know.

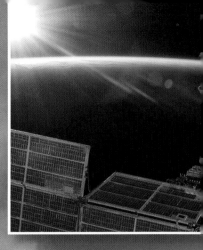

88 It took 88 space flights to build the fully assembled ISS.

2 Two spiders, Anita and Arabella, demonstrated that they could still spin their webs in space on the Skylab space station in 1973.

9 The longest a space walk ever lasted was almost nine hours. It was performed outside the ISS by Susan J. Helms on March 11, 2001.

90

For a space station in low-Earth orbit, the Sun rises every 90 minutes. This means there are around 16 sunrises and sunsets every day.

2

It took astronauts two days in a space shuttle from launch until docking with the ISS. It was not far, but they needed to match orbits.

6

This is the number of people that make up a full crew on the ISS.

19,000

By the end of November 2009, it was estimated that 19,000 meals had been served on the ISS.

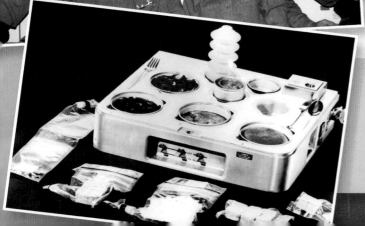

What We Learn from Space

With so much scientific study going on in space, it is inevitable that some of the results find their way back to Earth.

In fact, space exploration overall has greatly changed the way we live our lives, from how we make tennis rackets to how we test cars.

Liquid metal
NASA studied materials that were both light and super strong. They came up with "metallic glass," which has been used in sports equipment. Another new material is twice as strong as titanium, can be made without weak spots, and resists being deformed.

Self–illuminating materials
The ISS contains signs made of a self-powering substance. This technology has been used to create signs, such as exit signs, to be used in low light. The material lasts a long time, withstands fire and weather, uses no electricity, and needs no maintenance.

Artificial limbs

The science that helped space equipment last longer and keep astronauts safe is now being used to make better prostheses. This includes foams to make them more comfortable and real looking, diamond coatings to improve the durability of joints, and robotics to make them work more like real limbs.

Sunglasses

NASA created protective eyewear for their welders to protect against the light given off by welding torches. These same light-filtering dyes can be used to block glare in sunglasses, and make them scratch resistant.

Crash analysis

NASA created a camera-based tracking system to improve robotic assembly processes on the ISS. Car manufacturers now apply this technology to crash tests to help them see how crash test dummies are affected.

Glossary

air lock (AYR LAHK)
A chamber between the inside of a space station and the vacuum of space.

alloy (A-loy) A material that is the combination of two or more elements, at least one of which is a metal.

Almaz (AL-mahs) A series of space stations developed by the Soviet Union with a defense purpose.

astronaut (AS-truh-not)
A person trained to go into space.

booster (BOO-ster) An entire rocket, or sometimes a strap-on, that is used to get the space vehicle off the ground.

carbon dioxide
(KAHR-bun dy-OK-syd) The odorless gas exhaled by humans and many other animals.

cosmonaut (KOZ-muh-naht)
A Soviet or Russian astronaut.

decompression chamber
(dee-kum-PREH-shun CHAYM-bur) A room where the air pressure can be lowered.

International Space Station
(in-ter-NA-shuh-nul SPAYS STAY-shun) The space station that has been developed and used by many nations worldwide.

laboratory (LA-bruh-tor-ee)
A place where scientific experiments are conducted.

Mir (MEER) A space station built by the Soviet Union using an innovative modular design.

modules (MAH-joolz)
Individual units of a space station that are designed to be assembled with other units and work together as a whole.

ozone layer (OH-zohn LAY-er) The layer of the atmosphere that contains ozone, and which protects Earth from ultraviolet light.

pressurized
(PREH-shuh-ryzd) Made so that the pressure inside is higher than normal.

prosthetics (prahs-THET-iks)
The science and medicine of artificial body parts.

radiation (ray-dee-AY-shun)
Energy that moves in the form of waves or particles away from an energy source, such as the Sun.

resistance training
(rih-ZIS-tens TRAYN-ing)
Exercises that get the muscles to work against resistance, such as lifting weights or doing push-ups.

Salyut (SAH-lut) A series of space stations developed by the Soviet Union.

Skylab (SKY-lab) A space station launched and used by the USA.

solar panel (SOH-ler PA-nul)
A device used to capture sunlight and convert it into electricity.

space station (SPAYS STAY-shun) A permanent or semipermanent structure used for extended stays in space.

space suit (SPAYS SOOT) The suit worn by astronauts when they go outside the space vehicle on a space walk.

space walk (SPAYS WAHK)
The process of an astronaut
going outside of a space vehicle,
often for the purpose of repairs
and maintenance.

traction (TRAK-shun) The grip
of one surface to another.

ultraviolet light
(ul-truh-VY-uh-let LYT) Light that
cannot be seen by the human
eye and that is of higher energy
than visible light.

weightless (WAYT-les)
The apparent sensation of no
weight, or "zero gravity," when
an astronaut and space station
are both in a free-fall orbit.

Index

Websites

Due to the changing nature of Internet links, PowerKids Press has developed an online list of websites related to the subject of this book. This site is updated regularly. Please use this link to access the list: www.powerkidslinks.com/disc/space/